EMERGENCY
LESSON PLANS

Instant activities to use for any teaching emergency!

Concept: Geoffrey R. Lorenz
Author: Bonnie J. Krueger
Editor: Barbara S. Meeks
Cover and Book Design: Patti Jeffers

© 2009 Lorenz Educational Press,
a Lorenz company, and its licensors. All rights reserved.
Printed in the United States of America

ISBN: 978-1-4291-0392-3

BRIDGING
the Gaps in Education™
Lorenz Educational Press

P.O. Box 802 • Dayton, OH 45401
www.LorenzEducationalPress.com

National Education Standards Addressed:

Grades 1-2	Chocolate	The Earth	Farming	Pets	Pigs	Recycling	The Seasons	The Vikings
English:								
NL-ENG.K-12.1	X	X	X	X	X	X	X	X
NL-ENG.K-12.3	X	X	X	X	X	X	X	X
NL-ENG.K-12.4	X	X	X	X	X	X	X	X
NL-ENG.K-12.5	X				X	X		X
Mathematics:								
NM-PROB.PK-12.2	X		X		X	X		X
NM-PROB.PK-12.3	X				X	X		X
NM-PROB.CONN.PK-12.3	X		X		X	X		X
NM-NUM.PK-2.1	X		X		X	X		X
NM-NUM.PK-2.2	X				X	X		X
Science:								
NS.K-4.3	X		X	X	X	X	X	
NS.K-4.4		X					X	
NS.K-4.6						X		
Social Studies:								
NSS-USH.K-4.1								X
NSS-USH.K-4.4	X							X
NSS-G.K-12.1		X						
Technology:								
NT.K-12.3	X				X	X		X
NT.K-12.5	X				X	X		X

How to Use This Book

Have you ever wakened in the morning not feeling well? You have a terrible headache or the flu bug that has been going around has finally hit you. It's too late to find someone to take over your class so you HAVE to teach. Or perhaps you are pulled out of class for an unexpected meeting, assembly or conference. To temporarily fill in for you, where can you find simple lessons that are easy to use and take little or no preparation? You need activities that your students will enjoy working on while learning at the same time!

Welcome to *Emergency Lesson Plans*, a collection of educationally-based, cross-curricular activities that are ready to use for any emergency teaching situation. This unique selection of articles and non-fiction stories appropriate for specific grade levels can serve as a starting point for cross-curricular studies. They can also easily be added to existing classroom studies because of the wealth of subjects covered and their support of multiple National Education Standards.

It's always a good idea to have a backup plan, just in case the situation rises. Let these emergency lesson plans help you with those "I just can't teach right now" moments.

Table of Contents

From the Ground to the Dinner Table

Have you ever wondered where popcorn comes from? Where does the grain in your morning cereal grow? Are strawberries and bananas made at the grocery store? No – they all come from farms!

Many of the foods we eat every day are grown on farms. These farms can be very large and cover many miles. Some farmers raise animals like cows, pigs, and sheep. Most farmers grow different kinds of plants. These plants are called crops.

Farmers can grow many kinds of crops. These crops are used to make many of the foods found in grocery stores. Wheat is used to make bread and cereal. Corn can be made into taco shells. Beans are often put into chili. Some farmers grow apples, strawberries, and other fruits that can be eaten as a healthy snack.

After the farmer grows the crops, they need to be taken from the ground. This is called harvesting. The crops can be harvested by hand or by machine. Some crops will be taken to the grocery store to be sold. Others are taken to a factory to be made into foods like pasta and bread.

The next time you sit down for dinner, think about where your food came from. Which parts of your meal did a farmer grow? Which parts were made in a factory?

Hammy the Pig

"Come here piggy, piggy!" The farmer walked through the cornfield. "Where is that pig?" he thought. He looked in the sheep pen. He looked in the hen house. He couldn't find the pig anywhere. He looked in the old barn. A pile of hay in the corner seemed to move. The farmer pushed away the hay. It was the pig! It had been taking a nap in the barn.

This little pig's name is Hammy. He is only a piglet. He has floppy ears and soft, pink skin. He has a short, curly tail. Hammy has four toes on each foot. He only walks on the middle two toes. Hold up four of your fingers. Now push back the first and last finger. This is what Hammy's feet look like.

Hammy is a very smart animal. On hot days, Hammy rolls in the mud. Why would Hammy do this? The mud cools off his skin. Pigs cannot sweat, and summers are hot on the farm.

There are more than 300 kinds of pigs. They come in all shapes and sizes. Some pigs grow to be the size of big dogs. Other pigs can weigh 800 pounds. Most people think that all pigs are pink like Hammy. But pigs can be pink, black, white, or even red.

Hammy spends his days on the farm with the other piglets. He will soon grow up to be a big pig. He will always have his curly tail and floppy ears. He snorts at the other pigs. He takes lots of naps in the barn. Hammy is the happiest pig in the world!

Understanding What You Read

Circle the word that best fits in the sentence.

1. Hammy is a (blue, pink) pig.

2. On hot days, Hammy likes to roll in the (mud, snow).

3. Hammy has a (curly, spiked) tail.

4. The farmer found Hammy in the old (mud puddle, barn).

Tell Your Own Story

If you were a pig, what would you do all day? Would you take naps like Hammy? Would you play with the other farm animals? Write a few sentences about your life on the farm.

____

____

____

____

____

____

____

📖 Vocabulary Builder

An antonym is a word that means the opposite of another word. For example, "wet" is the antonym for "dry". Write down an antonym for each of the following words from the story.

1. curly _______________________________________

2. hot ____

3. smart _______________________________________

❓ Figure It Out!

1. The farmer at Hammy's farm had some coins in his pocket. He had 1 quarter, 2 dimes, and 3 pennies. How much money did the farmer have? _______________________

2. One day, Hammy rolls in the mud for 10 minutes. The next day, he has time for a 15 minute roll in the mud. How much time does Hammy spend in the mud on those 2 days?

   ____

3. If Hammy is 24 months old, how many years old is he?

   ____

Word Play

Unscramble the following letters to make a word from the story.

1. rnba _______________________________________

2. gip ____

3. udm ____

A Roll in the Mud

Help Hammy find his way from the barn to the mud puddle.

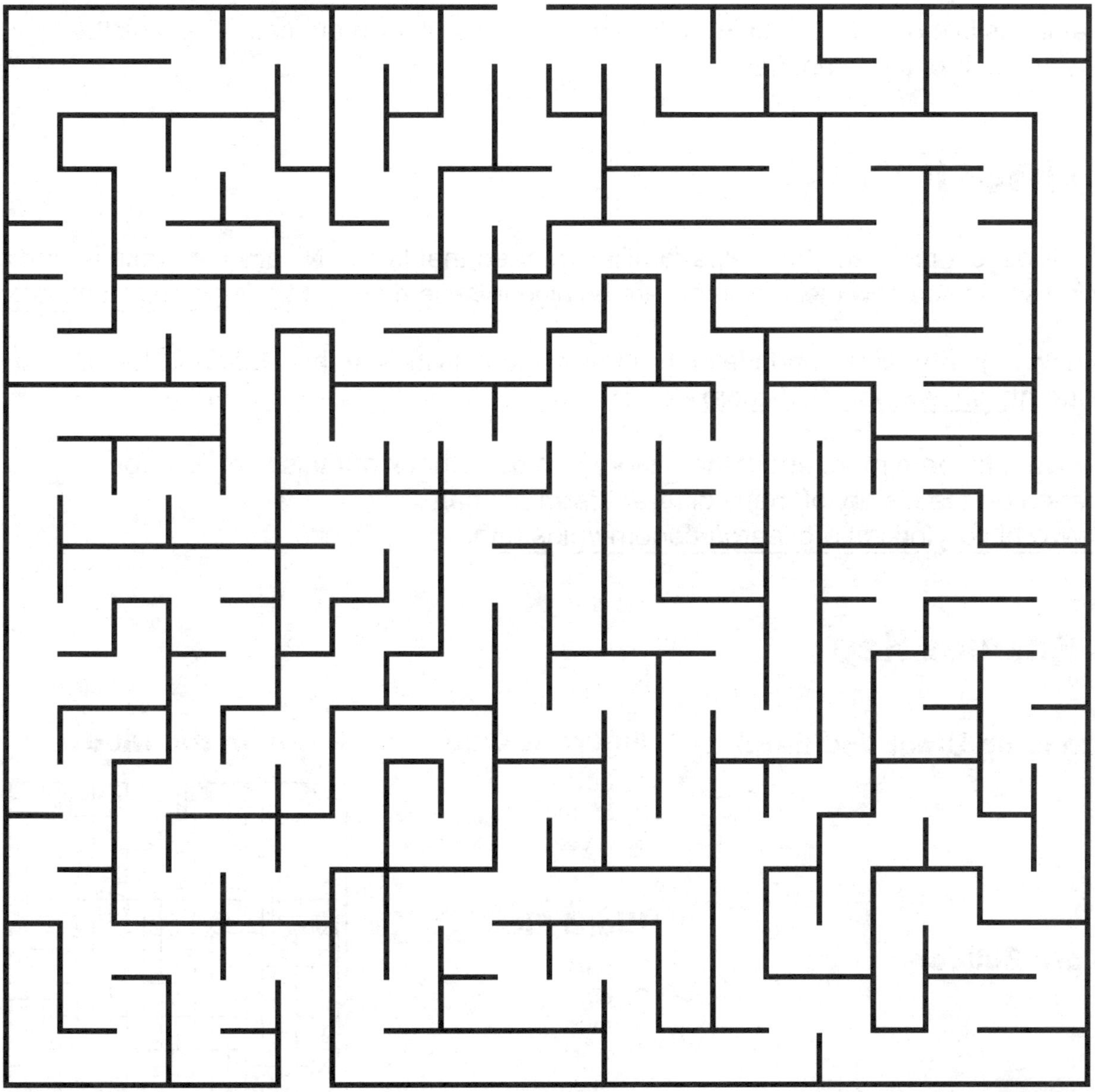

Start

End

Extension Activities:

Branching Out

1. Read "The True Story of the Three Little Pigs" by Jon Scieszka and Lane Smith to the students. This funny alternative to the classic kids' tale will have them laughing in their seats. How is this book different than the original story?

2. There are many different kinds of pigs that are raised around the world. Talk about the more common breeds with the class. Show them pictures and compare their colors, shapes, and sizes. How is one breed different from another?

3. Many animals live on farms. Talk about the other kinds of farm animals. Discuss the purpose of each of these animals.

Check It Out!

1. Pigs for Kids is a program that helps families in need that live in Nicaragua. Take a look at their Web site to see how these animals are helping to raise money. http://www.pigsforkids.org

2. Learn how pigs are raised and play fun games and activities at this National Pork Board Web site. http://www.pork4kids.com

3. Do you want to learn more about the history of pigs? Check out this Web site for information on the history of many different farm animals. http://www.historyforkids.org/learn/economy/pigs.htm

Answer Key

Understanding What You Read

1. pink
2. mud
3. curly
4. barn

Vocabulary Builder

1. straight
2. cold
3. dumb

Figure It Out!

1. $0.48
2. 25 minutes
3. 2 years

Word Play

1. barn
2. pig
3. mud

A Roll in the Mud

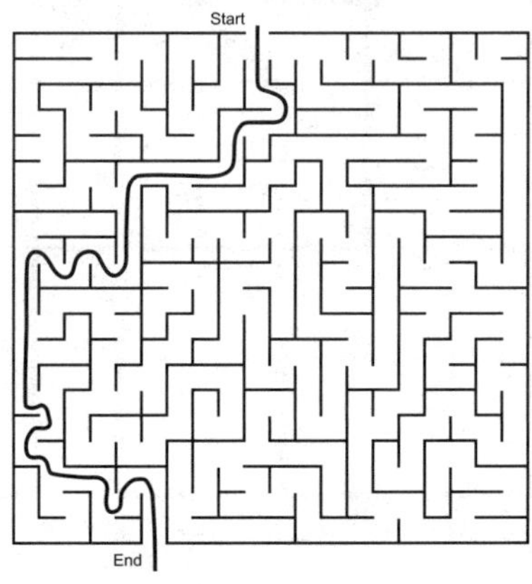

The Mighty Vikings

The Vikings lived many years ago, but stories about them are still told today. They were known as brave warriors. They were explorers who sailed across the seas. Many people feared them, but some were called heroes.

Vikings were known for being tough in battle. They often attacked nearby lands. They stole food and gold. They even stole people! Axes and spears were the tools they used to fight. Vikings could attack by land or use their ships to fight at sea.

Many Vikings were sailors. They built boats of all sizes. These boats used oars to move through the water. Some boats had up to 32 oars. The Viking sailors did not use paper maps to find their way. They looked at the stars. The stars acted as a big map in the sky.

The Vikings sailed to far away places to trade with others. Sometimes they found new lands.

Not all Vikings were sailors or soldiers. Most Viking men and women worked on farms. They planted gardens and raised cows and sheep. They made tools and pots over large fire pits. Many women wove cloth for clothes and blankets.

Viking children did not go to school. They learned from long stories called sagas. Sagas told tales of many Viking heroes. Some of these heroes became kings. Others found new lands. Imagine telling stories instead of going to school. It may have been fun to be a young Viking!

Understanding What You Read

Circle the correct word in each sentence about Vikings.

1. Viking boats used (oars , golf clubs) to help them move through the water.

2. Instead of maps, Vikings often used the (internet , stars) to find their way.

3. Most Viking men and women worked (on farms , in stores).

Tell Your Own Story

Some Vikings were known as fierce warriors. Imagine that you have grown up as a Viking. Draw a picture of yourself prepared for battle. Do you have an ax? What are you wearing? Be sure to give yourself a name fit for a warrior!

📖 Vocabulary Builder

How many syllables are in each of the following words from the story?

1. Viking _________________   3. stars _________________

2. attack _________________   4. trade_________________

❓ Figure It Out!

1. A group of Vikings sailed across the ocean in three boats. One boat had 6 oars, one had 10 oars, and one boat had 12 oars. How many oars are there on all three boats? _______

2. A Viking farm had 13 sheep. The farm next door had twice as many sheep. How many sheep did the second farm have? ____

3. A Viking traveled to another land to trade. A man offered to trade him an ax for 50 gold pieces. The Viking only had 41 gold pieces. How many more gold pieces would the Viking need to trade for the ax? _____________________________

🔤 Word Play

What is the plural form of each of the following words? Hint: if you need help, look back to the story.

1. person ____

2. child ____

3. sheep ____

On the High Seas

Complete the dot-to-dot diagram to find a common form of Viking transportation.

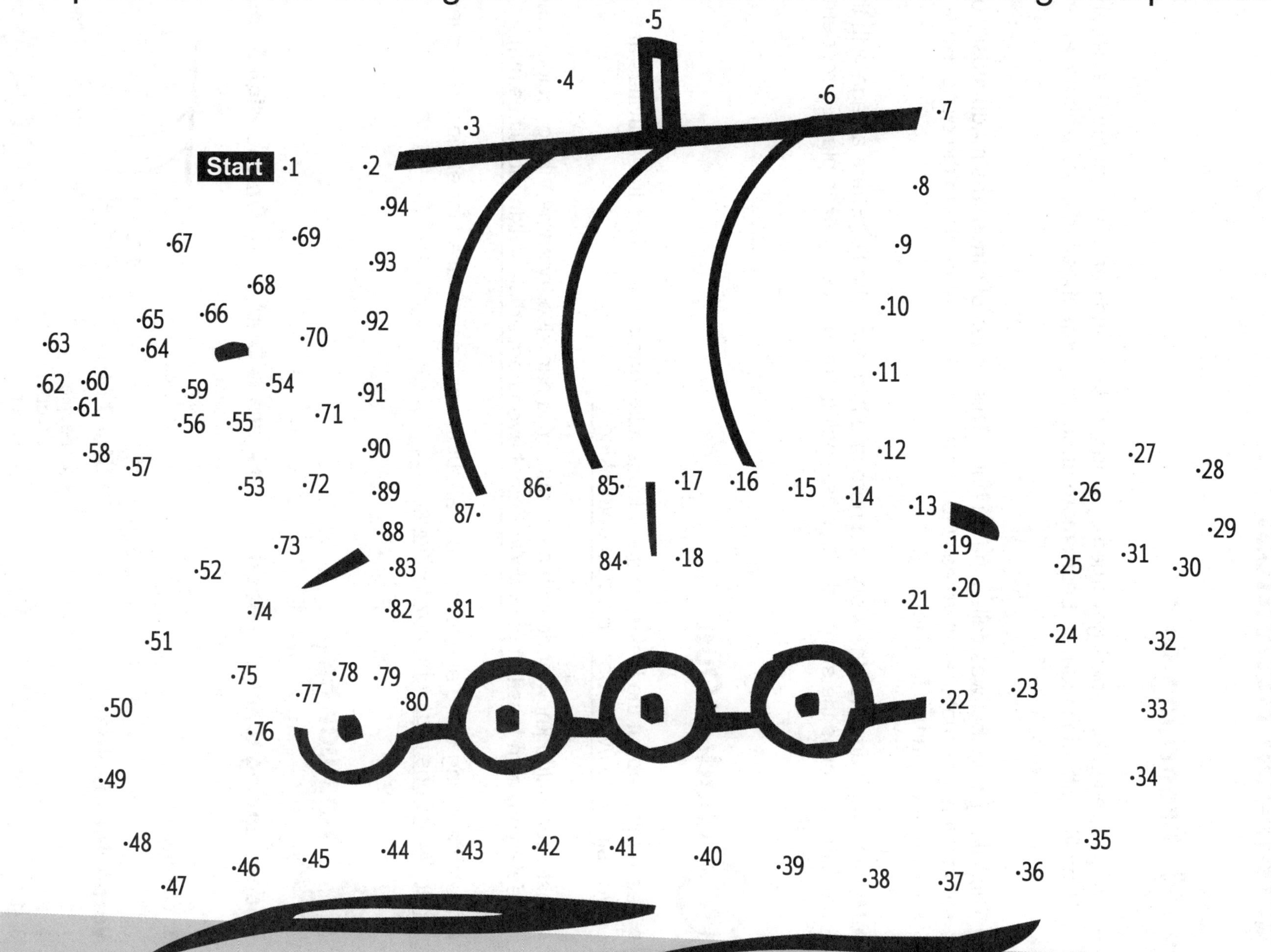

Extension Activities:

 ## Branching Out

- Vikings lived in kingdoms governed by kings, dukes, and earls. Talk about the hierarchy of Viking life with the students. Learn more about the large meetings, or Allthings, at which future plans were discussed.

- The Viking alphabet was called the Futhark. This series of runes was made mostly of straight lines so that they were easy to carve. Show this alphabet to the class. Have them spell out their names in runes.

- Many Viking sagas tell the story of a hero or a legendary battle. Share a saga with the students. Discuss the story with the class. Ask them to give an example of a modern day saga.

 ## Check It Out!

- Learn more about the history of the Vikings, play games, and find fun activities at this BBC Web site. http://www.bbc.co.uk/schools/vikings/

- Test your Viking knowledge with a fun quiz. You can also try some Viking recipes and create your own feast! http://www.learninghaven.com/articles/vikingactivities.html

- Watch a Viking video and learn more about the ships they used for exploring and in battle. http://www.pbs.org/wgbh/nova/vikings/

 ## Answer Key

Understanding What You Read

1. oars
2. stars
3. on farms

Vocabulary Builder

1. 2
2. 2
3. 1
4. 1

Figure It Out!

1. 28 oars
2. 26 sheep
3. 9 gold pieces

Word Play

1. people
2. children
3. sheep

On the High Seas

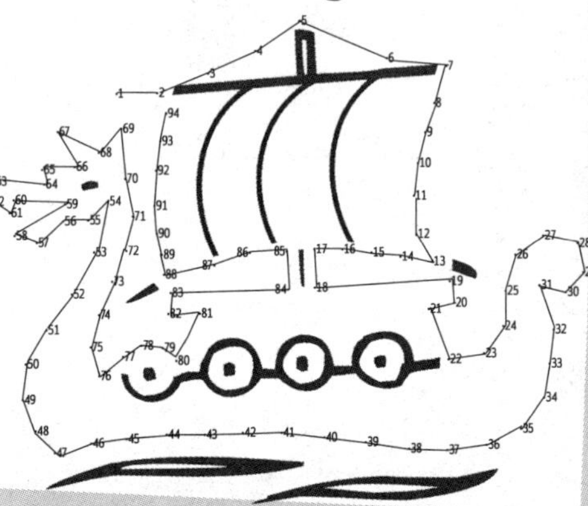

Do you have a pet? Maybe you have a cat that sleeps next to you at night. Maybe you have a puppy that likes to play fetch. You might even have a goldfish that swims around in a bowl all day. Even if you don't have a pet of your own, you probably know someone who does.

Dogs are a very popular pet. There are many different types of dogs. A Chihuahua is a very small dog, while a Great Dane may be bigger than you are! There are furry dogs and hairless dogs. Most dogs like to go for walks in the park. Nearly all dogs like to play fetch with a ball or a stick.

Cats are pets that love to cuddle. They often curl up into a ball and take a long nap. Some cats like to play with toys filled with catnip. You know a cat is happy when you hear it purring.

Many people have tanks filled with colorful fish. Some fish can be as bright as a rainbow. Crabs, snails, and small frogs can also live in these tanks. With a fish tank you can have a whole underwater world in your own house.

No matter what kind of pet you have, it is important to take

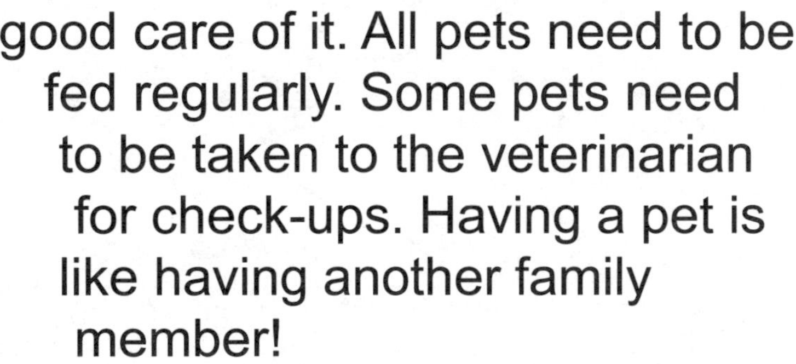

good care of it. All pets need to be fed regularly. Some pets need to be taken to the veterinarian for check-ups. Having a pet is like having another family member!

Extension Activites:

Humane societies are places where people can go to adopt animals that need good homes. Discuss with the students how humane societies help animals.

Dogs, cats, and fish aren't the only types of pets. What other pets do your students have? What are some of the strangest ones mentioned?

Veterinarians are very important people in pet care. What do they do to help animals? Talk about a career as a veterinarian.

Where Has My Little Dog Gone?

Oh, no! The dog has escaped from its leash! Find the dog by drawing it back on the leash.

Happy Birthday!

For your birthday, your parents gave you a new pet. What pet did they give you? Draw a picture of your new pet.

The Best Pet Owner

Match the pet with the things needed to take care of it.

The Sweet That Grows on Trees

It's the middle of winter. It is very cold outside. You and your friends have spent an hour playing ball in the yard. Your fingers are cold. Your ears are numb. When you open the door to your house, you smell something good. Your mom made hot chocolate!

Where does chocolate come from? It comes from a tree. This tree grows in the rainforest. It is called a cacao tree. A big fruit called a pod grows on this tree. The pods are hard and are the size of a football. Inside the pods are many beans. These beans are ground up to make a powder. This powder is used to make chocolate. It can take up to 400 cacao beans to make just one pound of chocolate!

Extension Activities:

Branching Out

- Barbara Barbieri McGrath and Jerry Pallotta have written several books that use chocolate to teach math. Check out *The M&M's® Addition Book* and *The Hershey's Kisses® Subtraction Book* for creative ways to incorporate a tasty treat into your math lesson.

- Have each student design a new kind of candy bar. They can write a description of their bar and design its wrapping. Have the class vote on the best new candy bar.

- Chocolate isn't the only sweet flavor used in cooking. Vanilla, caramel, and butterscotch are only a few other kinds of sweet tastes. Where did they come from? How are they used today?

Check It Out!

- The Field Museum's All About Chocolate Web page has many fun activities. Try chocolate recipes, work on puzzles, and even make your own chocolate online! http://www.fieldmuseum.org/chocolate/kids.html

- See how chocolate is made at the Hershey's® Web site. Explore the rest of the site to play games and learn more about the different kinds of chocolate. http://www.hersheys.com/discover/tour_video.asp

- Play lots of games with your favorite chocolate candies at the M&M's® Web page. You can even direct your own movie! http://us.mms.com/us/fungames/games/

Answer Key

Understanding What You Read

1. hot pepper
2. pods
3. football

Vocabulary Builder

1. cakes
2. beans
3. tree

Figure It Out!

1. 7 nickels
2. 6 pieces
3. 1,200 chocolate bars

Word Play

1. chocolate
2. fruit
3. spicy

The Sweetest Puzzle

BecaUse she Was a "cocoa nUt"!

Too Much Trash

Landfills are places trash is taken when it leaves your home. Have you ever seen a landfill? Garbage is piled high as far as the eye can see! The garbage sits in very big piles on the ground. The sun and wind break some of it down until it can be used by the Earth. This can take a very long time. Some trash does not rot or break down at all. It may be in the trash pile forever. What will we do when there is no more space for our trash?

We can help by putting less trash in landfills. How do we do that? We can recycle! Recycling is using something more than once. A lot of things that get thrown in the trash can be recycled instead. Paper, plastic, and metal are a few of these things.

Paper is made from trees. Millions of trees are cut down each year to make paper. This paper is thrown into the landfills as trash. The trees used to make paper are no longer alive to make our air clean.

Trees may also have been homes to animals. Recycling more paper means cutting down fewer trees.

Plastic is made from oil. It is used to make bottles and bags. Plastic does not break down in a landfill. A plastic bag put in a landfill today will be there a thousand years from now. You can see why it is a good idea to recycle plastic. This will leave less trash in the landfills.

Metal soda cans are very common. You may have some in your own kitchen. These cans add to the piles of trash. Recycling cans is very easy and can save a lot of energy.

What can you do to help? Many towns have places where you can drop off things to be recycled. Some cities give families bins for recycling. These bins are picked up with the trash and taken to be recycled. You can do your part to recycle.You can clean up litter or plant a tree. It is important to take care of the Earth now so kids in the future can enjoy it, too.

Understanding What You Read

Write whether the following statement is TRUE or FALSE.

1. __________ Plastic does not break down in a landfill.

2. __________ Paper is made from sand.

3. __________ Recycling is using something only once.

Tell Your Own Story

You have decided to help your town by recycling. What are you going to do to help? Are you going to save all of your soda cans? Are you going to pick up litter in your neighborhood? List two ways you can recycle in your town.

1. ____

____

____

____

2. ____

____

____

____

 ## Vocabulary Builder

Decide which of the following words are compound words. Divide each compound word into two smaller words.

1. landfill _______________________________

2. something _______________________________

3. plastic_______________________________

 ## Figure It Out!

1. It will take 3 whole trees to make the newspapers that are delivered to all the houses on your street. How many trees are needed to make the newspapers that will be delivered to all the houses on 4 streets in your neighborhood?

   ____

2. It takes 12 days for a piece of paper to break down in a landfill. It will take 10 times that long for a cardboard box to break down. How long will it take for the box to break down? _______________________________

3. Sam recycled 13 plastic bags on Friday, 6 bags on Saturday, and 10 bags on Sunday. What is the total number of bags Sam recycled?_______________________________

 ## Word Play

Unscramble each of the following sets of letters to make a word from the story.

1. rasth_______________________   2. ncas _______________________

3. repap _______________________

Recycling Word Search

Find all of the hidden recycling terms in the puzzle below.
The words can be up, down, forward, backward, or diagonal.

J A S P H E L C W E N
T Y L C L L A F B X X
W R P G W C N A G H P
E K A U Z Y D M A Y B
R P N S L C F M R D S
E R L U H E I E B P N
T N I A V R L T A A I
T J J G S V L A G P N
I M T Y M T P L E E T
L N I B F T I Q P R R
Q S W S I O L C L G M

Bins	Litter	Plastic
Garbage	Metal	Recycle
Landfill	Paper	Trash

Extension Activities:

Branching Out

- Find out about recycling programs in the community. Discuss ways that the students can recycle at home and at school.

- Materials that break down in landfills are called biodegradable. Talk about this process with the students. Why isn't plastic biodegradable?

- Trash isn't the only threat to our environment. Different forms of pollution can be seen every day. What other types of pollution can be found in your town? What are some ways that the students can help create a more pollution-free environment?

Check It Out!

- Learn how you can make a difference by recycling different materials. Be sure to check out the games and trivia section to test your recycling IQ at this Web site. http://www.ecy.wa.gov/programs/swfa/kidspage/

- Find out how to recycle in your own backyard and make fun holiday crafts with recycled items. http://www.dnr.state.wi.us/org/caer/ce/eek/earth/recycle/index.htm

- Find out how Dumptown turned into Recycle City at this Environmental Protection Agency Web site. http://www.epa.gov/kids/garbage.htm

Answer Key

Understanding What You Read

1. T
2. F
3. F

Vocabulary Builder

1. land *and* fill
2. some *and* thing
3. not a compound word

Figure It Out!

1. 12 trees
2. 120 days
3. 29 bags

Word Play

1. trash
2. cans
3. paper

Recycling Word Search

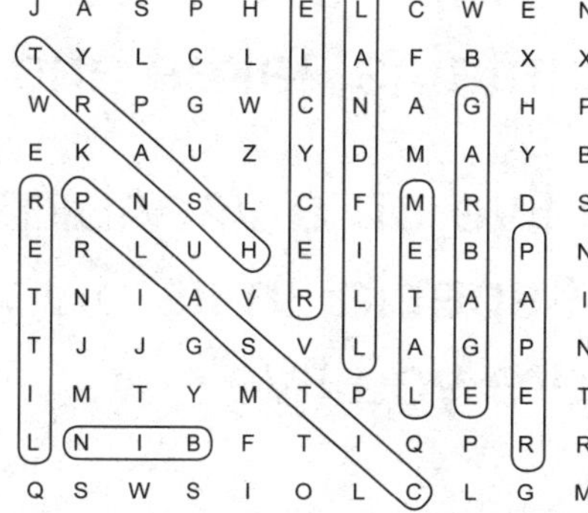

The Whole, Wide World

We live on the third planet from the sun. Earth is the only planet on which it is safe for us to live. There are many different kinds of life on Earth, including people, animals, fish, bugs, and even germs.

Our planet is covered with land and water. Some scientists think that all of the land used to be in one big piece. Today, the land on Earth is divided up into continents. There are seven continents. They are North America, South America, Europe, Asia, Africa, Australia, and Antarctica.

Each continent is divided into smaller pieces called countries. These countries are home to different types of people, animals, food, clothes, and even weather. In what country do you live?

How can you see these countries and continents? You can look at a map or a globe. A map of the world is a flat piece of paper that shows the continents, countries, and oceans of Earth. A globe is a ball-shaped map. Globes let you see the shape of the Earth. Some maps and globes also show mountains, lakes and rivers.

We live on a very big planet. Each part of Earth is different and special in its own way. What is special about the place where you live?

Extension Activities:

Examine a map of the world with the students. Compare the map to a globe. Do they both show the same features of the Earth? What are the benefits of each?

How are the other continents different from North America? What are the differences in climate, food, and native species? Which continent is the most like North America? Which has the most differences?

How are maps used in our everyday lives? What jobs require the use of a map? Find other types of maps you can share with your students.

Where In the World?

Follow the directions below to color the map of the world.

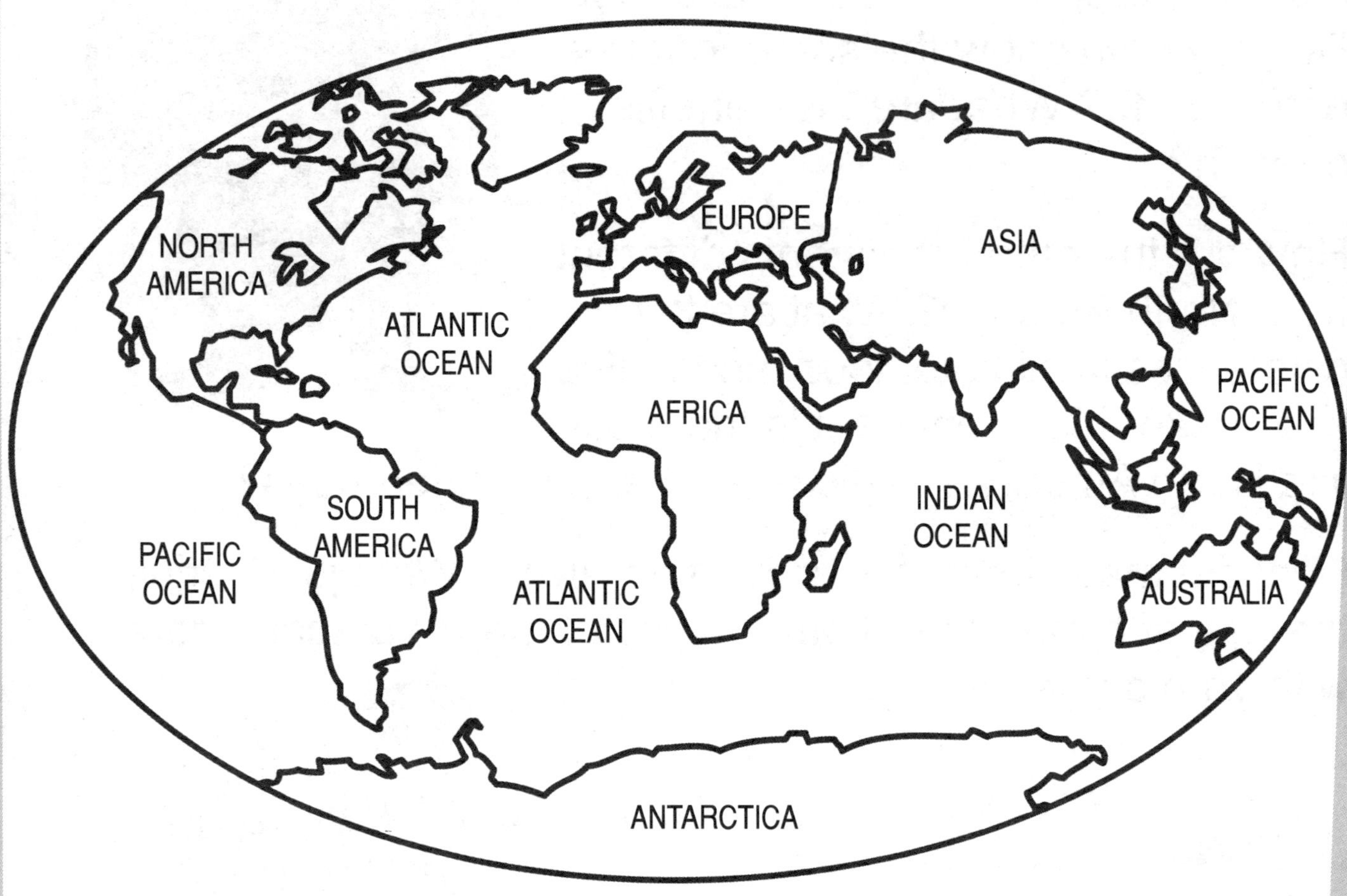

1. Color 2 continents RED.

2. Color 2 continents GREEN.

3. Color 1 continent ORANGE.

4. Color 1 continent YELLOW.

5. Color 1 continent BROWN.

6. Color all of the oceans around the continents BLUE.

Map It Out

Draw a map of your classroom. Be sure to label all the important places.

Animals Around the World

Draw a line from the animal picture to the continent where it lives.

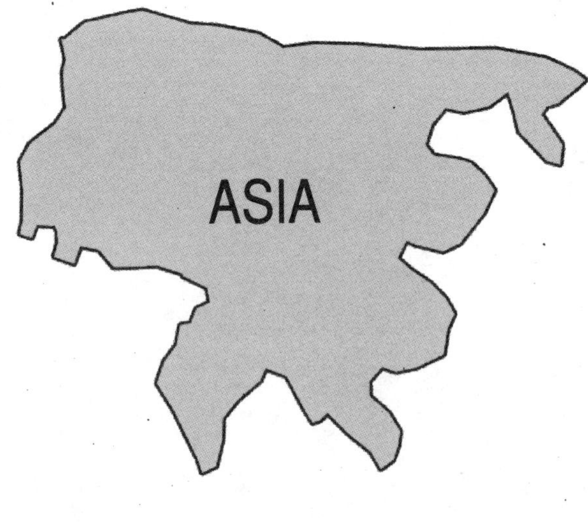